I Am Here

Poems by

Rosie Adamson-Clark

Peace, Joy + Light

2023.

Rosie. A-C

xxx

Ogygia βooks

Photograph of Rosie: Carole Martin

Front cover photograph: Leigh Carter-Shaw

I Am Here

Poems by

Rosie Adamson-Clark

I Am Here

Poems by

Rosie Adamson-Clark

Dedicated to John Cassidy, a fine poet and mentor, who died on January 23rd 2023.

Also dedicated to all the amazing staff at Bolton Hospice

Introduction

What a treat and a privilege to introduce you to this collection of beautiful poems by Rosie Adamson-Clark, my friend.

Rosie and I met first at the wonderful Bolton Socialist Club and bonded straight away over our shared love of art, theatre, poetry and music - and our shared activism.

Running through all that Rosie does is LOVE. Love for her darling Chris, the subject of more than one piece in this collection, and the quiet, steady, steadfast wind beneath her wings. Love for her friends and comrades. Love for art and nature. Love of this imperfect world and its people. As I write, Rosie is very poorly, and in and out of hospice care. It is fair to say that she is raging against the dying of the light. WIth depleted energy and oxygen, her body is a battlefield, but Rosie will not be vanquished: writing as though her life depends upon it. Not just poetry but film scripts (she has a body of work all of which endeavour to highlight injustice and inequality in one way or another), reflections on her Quaker faith, cards to friends, and letters to those in power - constantly and passionately holding them to account and calling on them to ACT - to save our NHS, to treat our refugees with the compassion they deserve, to make our services more inclusive to people from the LGBTQ community.

As she asserts regularly, there is much work left to do. Her words (and actions) will be her legacy.

Her poems, like those of her poetry hero Mary Oliver, are full of exquisitely observed moments of beauty in the every day, and full of heart. For there is no stronger, bigger heart than that of Rosie Adamson-Clark. We are lucky to have her.

Julie Hesmondhalgh

December 2022

Preface

These poems have been written over a long period of time. A large number have been written in the last 4 years since I was first diagnosed with end stage untreatable heart failure and I became a Hospice patient. My journey is nearly over now, but I wanted to use some of the work to support Bolton Hospice, who have kept me alive this long, I feel.

Many of the poems have been previously published in various publications such as
Orbis
Pennine Ink
Worktown Words
The Friend – the Quaker magazine
Reflections from Pendle Hill (magazine of Pendle Hill Area Meeting, Quakers)
Malvern Quaker meeting newsletter
Beverley Quakers newsletter

I thank the editors and publications for making my work more accessible. My apology if any have been missed.

The poem *I am here* was gifted by me as the Bolton Hospice poem to be read out at the memorial event each year for those already gone before us. We should never forget the dead or those no longer in our lives. We give such a lot to those around us, often without knowing how, or why, or when.

I thank Julie Hesmondhalgh for many years of wonderful friendship, and encouragement. She has been a great support.

I thank those who have helped me on my journey and thank Chris Chilton for helping with this publishing process. I especially thank John Cassidy, a fine poet and writer, who has encouraged me and helped in selecting these poems. Our journey goes back to 1991.

I hope you enjoy the reflections or images the poems may bring. The themes are similar for my poetry, films, scripts, short stories... inclusion, equality, awareness of difference and isolation. Universal themes... which relate to us all. In buying this book you are supporting Bolton Hospice as all proceeds go to them.

Thanks, too, go to
Bolton Socialist Club, Bolton Quakers / Friends,
Bolton Unison, and retired members.

Friends and family, who know who they are, who have never left my side over the years, giving love, encouragement and support.

Peace, Light and Love to you, and to all those mentioned above... and in my life now and previously, such as my sons Christopher and Thomas and their families.

Especially to my darling wife Chris, sweetheart this is for you, always with you.

Rosie Adamson-Clark, January 2023

Contents

I Am Here

I am here in this day,
for now, this is all I have,
your careful, caring hands,
attending to my needs
with compassion,
my hours contain a life time,
past stories to relay before
my relapse,
a repose and slumber
deep, unwakeful,
the hour will come when
I will never return to the *now*,

How can we help one another?
I fear for your burden,
as you carry me,
emotionally, physically...
as your touch soothes my pain,
my fear, my many bruises,
my yearning for more life,
or... less,
you tell me this is not a heavy thing,
in fact you came to the bedside
of the dying to sing,
whilst the sun shone,

or did it rain?
I felt that deep warmth and joy
of life again,
the comfort of knowing,
you have such passion in your role,
brings me the serenity to let
go, this is all I wish to say,

that dying is not to be feared,
here in this sanctuary, this
Hospice with love all around,
and all the respect for me,
the woman in the side room
filled with laughter and such love
and some tears,
as I tell tales of my interesting life,
though the letting go is easier for
some,

it comes to us all, the day the
fight is done, and we have had
that peaceful passing,
the good death,
because of you dearest
Nurse, Carer, Doctor, the
Worker who has given your time,
nurturing, and always love,

In that love… life goes on,
I know I will not be forgotten.

Ebb and Flow

The normal ebb and flow resumed,
smiles, whispers,
the loving tunes
hummed gently
as they decided on the day
ahead,
her soft breath on her lovers cheek,
eyes alight, they both say 'yes'
as they roll into the warmth of the bed,
she strokes the others hair as they dress,
remembering how it was so long
it caught under seats, arms, entwined bodies
in those early days,
a sensual trap, passion map,
an ocean of feeling,
glowing on a rainy dull day
which was not so drab,
one white haired now, both tired,
they look back on the journey,
two bodies...one mind she said
a slow steady stealing of hearts.

Falling

What was it nearly twenty
years ago that caught
my gaze, took my breath away
in between dusty tomes?

And so it began

the falling

Your eyes... did they really
meet mine as you instructed,
inducted the crowd of students
in your care?

What a falling was there

In that moment.

The brush of your hand grazed
mine, forever leaving its mark
behind, an indentation of flesh,
a bleeding wound

which said...

falling
your quiet seduction, magnetic,
the dawn to dusk longing,

my hand against your...
skirt... around,
falling... a slight sound,
down, down
like a star out of orbit

falling

falling in love,
dipping in,
sweetly... honey dripping
from the spoon,
hurry, hurry

falling in passionate lust
not knowing if you would come...
to meet me... soon, soon, sooner
don't stop,
don't stop...
falling

Did it take seven days
I wonder?

A revelation... God help me,
YOU
from dawn to dusk,
blessed art thou amongst women
Our mutual worship
flowed, wine and wafer,

I prayed for the hours,
the days, the nights,
my confession to you...

I think I am

falling

The journey begun,
descent, not decent
losing the old life,
stepping into new...
could we alter the

falling

the path of least resistance
was always loving you,
loss, let us speak of loss

falling

falling away, falling off,
masks dropped,
umbilical cords chopped
a bloody mess,
at times, our time,
torn from the heart
left... behind

the old life

Twenty years of falling

still falling
in love with you.

I Wake

I wake at 4am,
you sleep on,
the rise and fall
of your small form
under our covering
reassures me,
you will always
sleep well,
outside a wind batters
the May flowers,
baskets swing wildly,
auriculas beaten
down by hail and showers,
it is easy to be calm
in a rugged place,
you rise,
smiling at me,
a healing light
from your bright
loving face,
in this unseasonal
bleakness...
we are content.

Making Way For the Fall

She woke me,
though not as brightly as usual,
a half smile today,
another effort on her behalf,
but no beams behind
the greying sky,
I struggled to appreciate
her beauty,
through my shards
of pain,
would she lighten
my life fully,
my morning glory,
each day she has only
until the strike of the clock,
then the more solid noon
will step in, take over,
his heavy presence,
come heat or rain,
will tell me this day is half
over again,
perhaps as mourning
grows stronger,
she grows weaker,
a struggle to rise,
colder, more distant,
as thus an eighth
month beckons,

my beloved is more than half done,
in her eager greetings,
so she tires, and struggles
to emerge from rest
under the warm comfort
of a night covering,
soon she will not arise
with a spring, or energy,
much as I do,
we watch each other
grow feeble, doing our
best to stay bright,
no longer young

the effort not over
or done, but for others,
no surprise,
Summer nearly gone,
I await the dim light,
when renewal is done,
yes my love woke me,
but stayed not for long.

Pardshaw Quaker Meeting house

Smoke curling seductively
slowly snaking up the chimney
A charmer's basket opened
You broke twigs to feed the flames
Each snap an intake of breath
My heart was not at rest
The walls as thick as my arm
held no heat, icy
to touch, cold hands and feet
whitewashed, they kept out
the sleet on a cold November night
Quakers worshipped herein 1704
Solid stone floor
foot trodden, now foundation
for mattresses we sleep on...
No Light... only Silence.

Pebbles

You offered shining treasures,
a symbol of your love,
glittering jewels worn smooth
by the caress and lapping
of the water.
Silken speckled,
pale sugared almonds...
You invited me to drink
in the threads of fiery red,
and sunset yellow
like veins they stood out,
carried the pulse of 'life'
around the pebble when wet.
Damp Lake Garda kisses
as water licked the shore,
pebbles moving, chuckling
together, touching...
sensuous love tokens.

Same Skin

We wear the same skin
everything passionately fused... without
and within, beneath a landscape of
hidden, forbidden, contours
mirror contours, breasts rounded
and full, heaviness that falls
into soft hands eager to catch
what they already know
Silky, tingling skin... mine like yours,
hips that glide into hips, the jigsaw
of Mother earth meeting same, fitting
perfectly beauty and flaws
Our caress reassuring, perversely
alluring (so they say) exploring,
ignoring signs 'do not enter' and the exhilarating
'Danger within' but it's oh so right
because we wear the same skin.

Summer Liturgy MMMMMmmmm

Summer...
The heavy BUuuuuuzzzzzz
of the fat Bee
Honey, golden streams
sweetly spread
whilst I cradle and comfort
a fat blond June baby
warm fusion of desire
as we nurture each other...
he takes from my flesh
greedily... the slop, slurp
as he suckles, hungry
for my summer heavy breast
I take from him, touch,
unconditional giving, love
settling back on a lush
lawn, he fixes me with one blue
eye, the colour a small promising
plum on the laden tree
Summer... the heavy buzzzzz
of BEEing!

A Murmuration

Even in the dull February sky
the murmuration
swirling, swift, smooth,
created
wondrous movement
and if we looked slightly
askance,
the birds shaped
like figure eights, balloons,
and helix forms,
took on the kaleidoscope
changes of my childhood toy,
transfixed, stone statue
I broke the spell,
leaning into the camera
to capture the magic
of nature.

An Orchestra of Birds

She relaxed in the sun
knowing late spring
the season of fervent growth
had begun
to fill the garden spaces
flowering trees and eager shoots
reaching up towards
the traces
of jet stream
a higher meadow in blue sky
peacefully reclining
on a garden chair
she was serenaded by song
and music
an orchestra of the air

Cold Stone

Rattling, banging,
mournful sound,
a half broken gutter,
sobs constantly whilst
forming a wry smile,
at the dirty
pooling,
suffering on the mud
heaped ground.

Water seeps,
crying for help,
battering the siding,
stone building
in a wild grief,
seeking attention,
as it wails the lament
of the lost when none
is given.

From the muttering
of a hopeful snow flurry
in December,
the keening came to assault
hopeful changes,
and the wishes of the Happy
New Year,
were quickly replaced

with a heartless
waiting.

Morning comes but
momentarily,
ahh no respite,
no lighter warmed breeze
for outdoor dryings,
a plaint sob as people retreat,
pushed inside,
stone tears again,
only the planet can suffer more.

Cornflower

The azure centre
gazing out towards the greenery,
like an eye on a stalk,
curious,
startling,
ready to wink and entice
with its singular unique
beauty
It alone stands next to the hoary
old half eaten hosta
the slugs are not interested
In the remnants of their stalks
nor the optic slim thread
the one blue lens
appears to focus on our
sheer joy as we lean in to
touch and trace the gentle bloom
whilst slugs and snails can only
gaze on in envy.

End of the Day

I suppose it is nearly the end of the day,
what did I want from it,
now I cannot have it back,
this night,
I wanted, no needed to say,
you are beautiful, Mother nature,
so often ignored and made small
or slight,
but here I am looking at that last fading light,
the beauty takes my breath away,
did I do well in this nearly spent day,
did I reach out to admire your colours,
your land and sea,
your Motherly offerings, nurturing... not just me,
though it feels like it in the dusk,
the days are pulling back quickly,
the hours in each, I am told, do not change,
but surely they must,
I lust for more hours, oh please,
just to drink in your
beauty, your offering to us all,
but you tire too, not just me,
so you begin to fall,
shorter daylight, darker nights,
birds moving into autumn flights,
what can we do to help you stay,
stay healthy and strong,
love me more you reply,

just a little more each day,
be kind to my weary ebb and flow,
and leaves that droop,
scoop me up and feed me well,
earth and sea, and this the beauty
of my night sky,
once she fell... into my arms,
I will hold you up I cried,
and all others must too,
look around sky and sea
of deep, deep blue... for now.

Hardcastle Frogs

The cool skinned, emerald velvet frogs,
no longer a leaping, hot and fatigued
overhead sun beating down,
she who once jumped freely,
now disinterested in he who
lazily spawns.

Tiring, limbs locked, she
is now the jumped,
and he just begs a lift,
the slow dull male,
the eternal passenger.

He, just there for the bumpy hot ride,
from fence to stone, to garden compost,
abandoned last season, yet writhing with life,
all afternoon he shows
little interest in the where,
or why, and evidently not the how
of it all... for she will do the work.

They halt, with nowhere to hide,
dried skins, parched,
no root to squeeze under,
the sun an unremitting bright ball
in the noon sky.

She, unfulfilled, dry,

expires under his coupling
He, male sleepy, post coital
sated after all his lack of effort.

Hands gently lift the wearisome
honeymoon couple,
faces focussed, a child brightly
clad, excited at his find,
jabs a sticky finger in the mound.

The frogs, exhausted, focussed on
survival, she at least, will produce
the next generation of lazy male
and overworked frustrated females.

Humans it seems are not their main concern,
for frogs bereft of ponds to court in,
mud croak, slithering,
lose interest in their passion
they simply concentrate
on when to wander, when to jump
and return to dark waters.

Home to the Harbour Lights

Across the ink dark oily sludge,
it could not be called water,
surely not,
muck that flowed slow
as treacle from the dented
tin in our kitchen cupboard,
I had cycled out to the stone
steps to sit awhile,
pushing aside the old year,
welcoming the New as best I could,
tidal lapping at my good new boots,
I noticed the winking,
friendly like over the way,
first one side, then t'other,
off on, off on,
the harbour lights,
like two blinking eyes,
guiding vessels to safety,
never dimming,
on in all weathers,
welcoming water weary seamen,
smiles, relief to mirror the bright sparkle,
in the damp grinding cold of the night,
like stars in a moonless sky,
or a string of fairy lights on the tree,
chug, chug, as engines motored down,
the vessel arrived safely,
thanks to the guiding lights,

I turned the dynamo
on my bike and rode home
cheered by illumination
from cats eyes.

Hosta Grazing

The soil, warmed now by the bright
sun,
parted happily for the green erudite
probe, nose like, sniffing promisingly,
at the scent of growth in the air,
the viridescent
life pointing ahead, leading the way,
pioneer for the sister shoots
who in busy unison will salute the sky
for a short time
later, verdant borders,
lush, push, plush hosta, not dispelling foreign
bodies, all are welcome, slugs take note
the mice an invite to lunch here,
the greens before the beer which awaits
in the trap
Sward ravaged, though the tender
viridian ripple leaves some intact,
the copper of the steady slug
half hidden in sight as it munches
away... the resulting verdigris
all aspects of beauty for spring
and summer days... hosta grazing.

Pigeons

The pigeons are here again,
bloody things,
stealing the seeds left out
for birds with smaller wings,

less robust flighty friends,
they come in twos
disguised as some peace doves
who only bill and coo,

they bully the finches
robins and wrens
A gang of capitalist thugs,
feathered seed store pinchers

taking from the poor to line their
own nests
building their empires at other
birds' distress

Icarus and his sun reaching
limbs
flight territory
nimble beauty

They do not learn as we rush
at them, broom in hand
waving them off,
the disdain should be teaching

them
They are not wanted...
but...
back again they land

on the top of a thin icy pole
not liked,
not loved,
the pest from above,

the conservative pigeon...
seed stealer, food grabber
land lubber,
position cheater.

She Spins Slowly

Early morning walking,
on an isolated fell,
the air crisp and sharp,
on the windy moorland dell,
the rescue dogs bound ahead,
enjoy their first few laps,
vast expanse before us,
breath visible,
slowly exhaling,
heads covered by winter hats,
an orb spider has worked some magic,
her gossamer threads on show,
a weaving of survival,
an intricate silvery tale,
each day starting anew in gales
and frost and hail,
she spins each lifeline slowly,
each thread connecting weft,
dew heavy,
a mark of nature's success.

Sit

Exquisite like velvet,
soft and lush,
it's startling vibrant
green
at odds with the slow
easy comfort of its surface,

sit,

observe its blending,
with the stone hard wall,
it teased its way onto,
a cold unbending,

place,

the two materials,
rock and succulent
lichen,
create the perfect seating
after a tiring walk,

easy,

here looking
at the beauty,

the weary feel refreshed
by nature and her kindness.

Snow and Dust

Trees standing sentinel
A dusting of powder snow
Sugar sweet the winter scene
on the Swiss chalet below

A sparrow hawk
Wings effortlessly beating time
Creating tremors of hoar frost
as voles hurry by
unmoved by the season's beauty
as they prepare to die
in the chill and raw.

The Treasure Field

The long walk, through the dense tapestry
of bracken and brush,
conducted in human silence,
though the birds cheekily chirruped
constantly over head,
the intense heat,
brought a sweat to our bodies,
which were swathed in many layers
to protect us from the fight which lay ahead,
we had gone prepared,

plastic bag heavy with garden gloves,
nestled against the secateurs
and plastic containers,
empty shells ready to be filled with the bounty
of the bramble bushes,
eventually, having fought our way well into
a deep tangled corner of the field,
we paused, panting, struggling to catch
our breath, out of condition I gasped,
stillness seemed to descend for a few seconds
after a fugue floated around us,
as the oppressive thrum,
and buzz of the insect life
made itself known to us two
intruders,
heart beating hard against my chest,
I paused to rest against my sticks,

a droplet of sweat ran down my cheek
as a wasp, uninterested in my presence
gorged itself on the over ripe fruits,
a semi-fermented late lunch,
alcohol aromas hanging just in front of my nose,
the omnivore, hic hic, buzzed around drunkenly
as it flew in a zig zag display,
leaving us to take the just ready fruits it did not
wish to drink from,
an abundance of berries
seemed to fall gratefully into the empty containers,
time slowed, as we concentrated on this small
patch of deep succulent growth,
the interior heat intense,
humidity making it hard to draw breath,
as we fought our way back out of the jungle,
bag and containers heavy with the dark
gold, we Incas returned home,
laden with treasure
soon to become a piquant blackberry jam.

Walking by the canal

Sunlight falling on the oily
black water,
shards of light,
splintering,
where once bicycle frames
and shopping trolleys
held aloft by rotting planks,

now, dredged clear,
as clear as mud can be,
fish began to make a return,
and old couples, walking,
along the rutted towpath,
strewn with cans and bottles,
needles in places,

wildflowers,
desperate to reach up past debris,
to grasp at the sun,
entice bees and some small birds,
whilst boys in gangs smoke weed
wafting on the spring breeze
it does not choke the flowers
as some weeds do,
a heady fug floats away
under the bridge.

Winter Watching

Hoar frost,
petrified hedgerows,
shivering, crow
alert guarding
country lanes,
hidden from all
but local view.

A tired sun
gentles the winter
mist along,
beckside,
sheep gather in tightly
knitted formation.

While resting
on an icy pole,
a falcon scans
the white flatlands
for lunch,

and, finding none
he turns his gaze
to infrequent
beetling traffic.

Woodland Walking

Early morning,
the heat just enticing the earth
into wakefulness,
the day soon unwraps
the bounty of nature,
I lean into brambles
and hand thick stems
of balsam,
I feel more alive than
ever,
the only sounds are my
laboured breathing,
and the caw of crows
or is it rooks, I am never
sure, the slow sultry
buzz of a half drunk
wasp filling my ears,
as I reach into the
woody undergrowth
to the rich glinting
black fruit,
as I pick, the juicy bulb
falls to the ground,
I swear it was protected
by the densely woven
leaves and branches,
I gather, one for me and one for the wildlife,
that's fair I thought,

as I breathed in greenery,
sap dripping, sweat gathering
on my brows,
blood pooling in the deep scratches,
these scars my badge of
dishonour for robbing
from an open air pantry,
I guarantee if you go
walking in the woodland
all life is before you,
the walk home will be
short, the memories long.

Woods at Night

The silent swoop of the owl,
brushing past tree tops,
skimming, slicing arms of the gnarled oak,
skittering wood mice and voles,

a distant coughing bark
of the fox as he scurries
back into the bracken...
waiting...

An ambush as badgers, badgering
the earth into small mounds,
finding tasty morsels
before disappearing back into holes,

the metropolis of the woods at night.

After She Was Gone

I got there as quickly as I could,
his eyes though blank, gave me a look,
which said 'yes it's true, she has gone',
he was kneeling on the floor,
clothes and beads hanging out of the wardrobe door,
from which he had pulled the flimsy rails
down, to smell the dress and a pink blouse,
sobbing silently he scooped up her essence,
doused his loss in her musk,
I wailed, loud and long, it couldn't be this way,
she had not been old, sixty six and nineteen days,
I don't think he really, truly cared,
a marriage of emptiness,
he had his difficult ways,
but no one dared suggest such a thing.
The funeral was bleak,
I stared at a plastic flower display
and rocked like a child,
Father said tears were weakness,
my sister mouthed the words of the hymn,
no words came out,
someone said it was important to show willing for
HER,
as for Father, she said she wanted to ghost him
years ago, "What's that?" I asked leaning into her
warm shoulder,
"it's what my last boyfriend did to me, just

disappeared
as if he hadn't existed, as if we had never been",
she moved about on the old creaking,
wooden crem chair,
which was obviously rotten,
it had supported hundreds of grieving people
many with fat bottoms,
"Mother will be toast now!" she whispered, watching
the curtains close in front of us, whilst
they played 'Amazing grace',
I was glad to get back to the parental bleak house.
Much later,
sitting on the floor by her wardrobe,
as he had done,
a sudden waft of Chanel scent,
Ma was with me now,
feeling my pain and helplessness,
she was not ghosted,
I could feel her hand stroking my hair
as I howled and keened,
my shoulders heaving in time to her light touch.

Beach Night

I think you told me about the night time swims,
the cold sea, calming after a hectic day,
it offered no danger you felt,
only a sort of silky, salty easing of the pain

you felt at the sadness in the world,
I asked why wait for night,
and who would rescue those in distress,
a beacon, you said, the sea is a beacon

and the distress just goes, it matters not which
way the tide flows,
perhaps the people in the tiny boats,
just plastic, barely able to float,

felt that too, the easing of their hunger,
hope returned, so the few who survive
such a journey can feel the draw of our land,
with or without a welcome to hand,

all that in your nighttime swim my friend,
you feel not loss, not an end,
but a drawing of a tidal pull, ties to their country
cut, the welcome of the colourful beach hut...

and the care and love of those who know,
sea swimming isn't all for show, or health,
or creating waves, it's to feel the element
which can end lives, but also saves.

Day at the Beach 1964

The journey to the beach
a rickety motorbike and sidecar,
her arms around his waist tightly,
as far as she could reach,
goggles and cap,
hiding piercing blue eyes
and blond hair of the
head of the household,
a very difficult chap,
always in control,
he would push us three
children into the sidecar,
elbows in faces and dead legs
my sister would bawl
that she couldn't see,
Paul was the youngest
and always wanted a wee,

finally the bike came to a halt,
juddering over, and roaring now
ceased,
the sand, right there for us to
run wild on, released,
Mother, headscarf on and coat
buttoned up,
got out the flask for tea to be supped,
the sandwiches shared,

with adults and children,
we huddled, shivering,
away from the crowds,
behind the sand dunes,
Mum's small transistor radio
belting out Beatles tunes very loud.

I Sense Green

Dark earth,
heavy clods,
uncleaving under
his garden fork,

Grandpa was a dour
grumpy man,
mean with his time,
very little laughter or talk,

we stayed well away,
until he went out back,
cap on head,
a bag of sour sweets

to dip into,
a contradiction like himself,
I don't think he had a garden plan,

maybe in his head,
weeds outed, manure
laid on top of his roses,
he grew fruit,

we could only steal
berries and rhubarb
as he didn't believe
in treats,

until he saw the new
green shoots emerging,
so pleased was he
for that moment,

we could choose
from his private bag
of delights,
I loved Spring!

Liminal

The back room... Grandma's domain,
she pored over the pots and pans
on the stove
as the newly pummelled bread rose
in the warming cabinet,
ready to place on the bottom shelf

she would delve into the dark interior
to grapple with dishes of bubbling
delight
Grandpa was assigned the other room,
sitting in front of the telly day and night,
he had little interest in her alchemy,
he loved the freedom,

not allowed over the threshold
he grumped and growled,
if he dared wander towards
her realm,
she would say scowling,
This isn't right,
Tommy I need the space,

he was cowed
she was warmed by heat
from the range
she ruled over the warm fuggy place,

the glow from the oven piercing
the deep gloom, Catherine the creative,

my position was liminal, hovering between the two,
I wanted to please Pops, but have Granny's
love in a cake tin too,
the door, an access to kitchen and lounge
a portal... heavenly threshold,
delicious smells wafted through
Grandpa changed channels incessantly,

it was something to do,
she stirred it up in a big brown bowl,
I licked the mix, loved them both
a youngster caught between two worlds
a hungry kid that's all!

Mother Love

The warmth of the kitchen wrapped round her as she worked,
Soft and pleasing like her old green winter coat,
She moved slowly, precisely, always humming, fingers drumming,
A handful of this, a measure of that,
Our pleasure came from watching her create
Love in a bowl... or dish,
Hidden behind that curtain sash, our excitement would rise

Steadily,

Steam, sultry and heady, relaxing to breathe in, coating pans and skin,
windows tightly shut to keep out the cold,
as she enticed the butter to melt, the scones to drop, the egg to fold,
beating the dough on the cold marble slab, slap, slap, magician's handsome
bread fingers, bread bap, red fingers slap, slap,
Chains of Mother love.

My Father

A tree of a man they said,
like a mighty oak,
which didn't bend in the wind
when,
finally rigid bough broke,
the end came suddenly,
a fall.

Bones shattered,
his trunk,
once the solid core,
of this upright difficult man,
no longer stable,
alone in some arboretum,
an orchard of wizened
non- fruit bearers,
antiseptic, sad cul de sac where
the old and damaged go.

Air,
stale and fuggy,
filled with
rapid scattered thoughts,
muttered and mumbled,
like leaves dropping
randomly,
gnarled and twisted,

the sap gone,
no longer rising
to meet the challenge
that life in a crowded
'would he, wouldn't he'
world brings.

The Drift

When did it happen,
the drift,
along the shore
We walked, looking
for bits of treasure,
saving almost everything,
Mother called it thrift,
which was also the name
of the store on the corner.

A simple time, small joys
were ours,
I once found an oar,
boatless,
not something I had seen
before,
I took it as mine,
dragging it home
spoils of the coast,
not sure what to make
of the treasure,
I parked it against our
broken fence.

Stroking it for pleasure,
would it capture my heart
now, the object

or the activity...
Shaking sand from my clothes
I realised all things
needed to change.

Air

You lay below on the wheezy
airbed,
it seemed to gasp as you rolled
over towards me,
reaching up to take my hand,

this wasn't what we planned,
the Nurses, moving glider like,
attended to your needs...
as well as the dying,

the dead peacefully tucked
up safely for the night,
strange how people no longer
say the word,
a harshness to it that lasts,
society prefers the anodyne 'passing'
or ‘past’... that isn't right,

berthed beside each other,
as it were,
was it a water bed?
No it was air,
ships in the night,

we seemed scuppered,
I heard you shiver, gulp,
trying to weep silently,
your small body heaved,
air escaped the temporary
resting place,

small life raft,
down the hall someone
sneezed,
then a long rattle,
climbing over the ugly cot sides,
your knee, or was it mine...

stuck in your nightgown,
why is dying so graceless,
me helpless, infantile needing,
we held on,
finding a small space beside me,
was it hope?

Kissing your salty tears,
pecking your cheeks,
I chipped away at your
outward calm,
togetherness,
I whisper...

'what will we do?'

A small, thin voice replied
'go on, we must, a 2nd chance'
balm to my ears and damaged heart,
but no, not that,
surely there are only first chances,

Here, this morning,
a fresh day to go fill,
precious time, I lasted the night
death did not rub me out,
beep dit dit trill of the machine,

the nurses in scrubs, busy now,
window opened to let in a fresh day,
I watched your eyes flutter,
hair ruffled by cool air,
cheeks brushed by my warm breath,
still here... yes still here,
second chance love.

Magicians at the Podium

Slowly,
people emerged from behind
closed doors,
urged on towards
normality,
when none was there,
the rules,
rewritten,
made little sense,
the new economy,
fear,
no helium balloons,
or kissing strangers,
the year Vera Lynn died,

encouraged out of hiding,
The battle quietly raged on,
scientists shook their heads,
politicians continued to smile,
bending the truth,
pulling rabbits of out thin air,
they encouraged us to
celebrate,
long before the feast was ready,
those at the bottom table
left out of the planning,
gazed at empty plates

where food should be,
no streamers here,
bowls empty,
no sharing the loving cup,
punch gone.

Oil for Balm

Darkened just enough,
the room is cool
against the midday heat,
settled on the bed,
head supported,
sandals removed from
my feet,
I sigh, relax,
just a little,
relieved to be cocooned,
I know I will feel
transported soon,
by the skill of your hands,
what else is here?

Intrigue, anticipation,
sometimes laughter,
after the end of the pulse
of pain,
finally I feel free, less hurt,
Frankincense smells drift
from the mix in your hands,
once again we talk
of plans,
for any remaining time,
long before I feel its
unctuous liquid on my skin,

my tired body,
heavy legs begin
to just...
relax,

I smell that woody
historic odour
I am able to imagine
a scene...
Was it really offered in a stable,
warm straw, hot breathe
on a cold night, exotic oils,
sanctuary...
I am able to relax,
in this room,
soon,
I feel spoiled by your touch,
I do not wish the end,
you apply just the right
amount of pressure,
not too much,
and then, kindly,
your face searches mine
for a signal,
I relax,
now, the long, slow, strokes

begin, lovingly applied again,
I relax,

just enough,
the oil feels sensuous,
calming, not rough,
not old as its smell suggests, so...
I relax,
like a rhythmical lullaby,
it encourages me to let go,
give in, cry if I want to,
only you and I will know,
sighing,
I relax,
my eyes will eventually close,

I know my time is nearly done,
I shall relax,
deeply, sweetly, until the next time,
when the treatment hour
has come,
your hands give respite,
prolong life, your gift to me,
your time, your warmth,
spirit and care,
no wise men 3 with this
offer of precious oil,
a comfort knowing your
wish for me,
causes not toil,
but a gift of skills,
a giving,

easing pain, suffering
ending life's ills,
you miss nothing,
so...
I relax,
staying focussed,
I am thankful you are here,
having this vocation,
we both relax as I leave the space...
able to smile again.

A Child Came to Meeting

A child came to Meeting,
a bright light shone,
he clapped at Ministry
and marched up and down
worries had he none.

Curiosity and energy were his,
his innocence engaging,
smiling widely at the gathering
darkness all gone,

listening as people spoke
he seemed to know
the Light was in this room
a beacon of hope.

Jumping for joy, he chuckled aloud,
like a bright warm sunshine
pushing back the threatening cloud,
Samuel brought love to the silence
as Quakers should do,
that child brought vibrancy
for me and for you.

Incurable

Racked with pain I surface again
Somewhere down the street a kid's
yelling at a yapping dog;
disturbed,
I move my head on the sweat-stained
pillow and belch gently.
Even in near death I'm striving
for the status of a Lady.
My Mother always claimed I'd never
make it, as she surveyed the pyramid
of wet tissues on the floor:
But that was years ago
I wondered what she was doing now
in her sixty seventh year,
still knitting jumpers with baggy
necks and bog roll covers I'll bet,
and patronisingly calling everyone 'dear'.
Angrily,
I thumped on the drool marks on the lumpy
pillow again. The sweat in rivulets between
my breasts and legs sapped my energy,
as it flowed easily to join the other bits
of me the bed contained.
Yesterday's bits of stuff
Nails,
as sharp as those in my coffin,
hiding in the folds and waves of sheet,

waiting to draw blood from my thin legs,
to add to the rest of the mess.
Twelve o'clock DF118 taken
I'm drifting off to the land of health
and laughter again, I'm twenty two
lying on some hot beach where I'm caressed
by warm rain; as it gently runs itself
around my firm brown body,
I drift, enjoying all the guys looking
at my supple supine loveliness,
and way down the beach, faintly through
the sound of the surf, I hear the kids
playing ball with some dog,
and I know everything's okay.

Passage on the Welfare State

The couple in the flat below sleep
until 3pm, there's no rousing them
when the sirens come on another
futile call.

The flat's in her name, the housing
pays, they both draw income support...
job seekers allowance it's all the
same

it's spent on beer and `E` and
coke, not the kind in the bottle,
it's no laughing matter, no fabulous
joke

she yells at all the kids in the street,
has tattoos on her hands and feet,
I'd never seen that before...
his nose is non-existent, broken too

many times to repair, looks like he walked
into a DSS door, he batters her black and blue
She's a cow he shouts... nothing the neighbours
can do

they party until 3am
let in friends to shout and drink
and fight again, it stops the boredom
setting in

the welfare pays, it's pretty grim,
she keeps her head down... loath to grin
she's lost more teeth, *It's the Government's fault*

he growls this out to assuage his
guilt, splattered statement with the
word 'fuck' inbuilt to emphasise
the urban tragedy.

Resuscitation

Travelling on the blue glide bus
that early morning rush
of shoppers, and grey faced, old before their time
workers,
manual dirt diggers, crammed into shabby
seats against the benefits claimants,
some shirkers and shifters, the old woman whispered
as two youths with a child in a pram wheeled
into her varicose veins;

the whoosh of the airbrake, a tired slow sigh,
vehicular fatigue,
as the terminus is reached at 9.45 and the 9.50
outbound is ready
for the next intake, she quickly speeds by,
I stretch and I struggle to stand shakily,
nodding my thanks to the red faced driver,
journey completed, my shopping bag in hand;

the ant hill like village, quite busy today, stone fronted
shops
and colourful eateries, the greengrocers side window,
full of winking primary colours, old fashioned heavy
scales laden,
now which way I ponder, perhaps down to the
railway, the steam
trains shunting and snorting impatient to depart,

ready, ready, ready,
iron visions of some ancient farm horse stamping the wet earth,
clumsy great beast, I seem to stumble, feet of clay,
heavy in spirit I drag
myself into the warm steamy cafe;

sniffing the gently rising wood smoke, curling like fingers, beckoning
this way and that,
ohhh odalisque incense,
enticed in by the rich brown smells,
bubbling black coffee, oven warm pies, my taste buds tango as I order
my food, sipping a welcoming warm drink, I know it's all good and relaxes
the body... I think,

the rhythms of life unhurried by change, you said 'routine is comforting'
"now tell me your name?" as you sat down beside me, ignoring the empty
tables, what beguiling blue eyes, I wanted some silence, not this jawing on fancies,
and slices of small talk, but here be the old folk daydreaming in reflective windows,
watching the world go by

I take a long, slow slurp of the Java as I gaze up the street, past well worn cobbles
flowing like lava, and the florists, aflame with the blossoms, how the land lies,
I realised I miss you, my darling, my love, I'm still looking in crowds,
gone,
but still strong is my hunger,
then way in the distance, a speck, I notice the slow walk, a strong steady gait, a masculine step,
the fair hair is moving with the speed of his stride, I long to wave at him, I catch, I fall, I glide,
I stop... my breath is all
gone...

will he take my heart and massage it in his hand, I shake myself
out of the dough like state, I am
risen back to life, as I sip the cooling coffee... a former lost wife.

The Slow Spelling Tango

The words on the page,
are dancing the tango,
dipping and diving,

as I try and catch their
meaning... double meaning,
as they blur, or misplace
themselves,

No orderly line for this
little band,
words like rabbits in
Alice land,

pop up, slip out, escape
my hand,
as the pen and I/eye do battle,

ringing, rolling, words
that rattle, prattle
in my head,
my eyes read 'dabble'

but I know it is/I am
addled,
I'm not disabled,
                    just 'dys' labelled.

Lean In

One stood out
from the woodland crowd,
huddled together,
seemingly
tired and cold
after the long winter,
thinly they reach
out towards each other,
comfort isn't the reason,
survival,
the less nimble, who
cannot bend,
whipped and lashed,
will come to a splintering
end,
cracking under the weight
of weather, not leaves,
she stands front facing,
like the ballerina,
prima,
positioned to catch
the nourishing rays,
every light droplet
taken in,
it's worth leaning into
the brutal winds

to grow ruggedly,
on into another year,

Lean in, lean in.